I0169664

HOW SMALL WE ARE,

HOW LITTLE WE KNOW.

Alexandra Melville is a writer and teacher. She was highly commended in the Forward Prize and is published in the Forward Anthology 2022. Her poetry has appeared in publications such as The Rialto, The Moth, and The Interpreter's House among others. She was longlisted for Live Canon's Poetry Prize 2020 and received special mention in Against the Grain's Poetry Competition 2019. She has an MA in Creative Writing and Education.

ISBN: 978-1-915079-54-1

Cover designed by Aaron Kent

Edited & Typeset by Aaron Kent

Broken Sleep Books Ltd
Rhydwen
Talgarreg
Ceredigion
SA44 4HB

Broken Sleep Books Ltd
Fair View
St Georges Road
Cornwall
PL26 7YH

Contents

how small we are, how little we know.

Alexandra Melville

You could see us falling even then.

I'm wearing the net curtain from Premier Inn's window
      like a veil. I'm eating Greggs from the bag.
      All the people below the glass roof are
            walking as though they are not incredibly small,
            riding the mall escalators down from floor to floor
                  as if they're not endlessly falling. As if they'll never

wear no knickers and eat ring doughnuts
      in front of an 8th storey window,
      rolling gold zeros over the carpet.
            The couples are holding minute hands, swinging
            the club of their fists back and forth
                knocking all comers out of their path.

The lighting in Premier Inn is particularly unflattering.
      I'm unlikely to find true love again
      in this light. If I turn it off, the pane flickers
            from sticky-fingered mirror to city at night.
            And the glass roof lights up like a yellow road,
                staggering all the way to a gold, unveiled moon –

    full and calm
        as a guidance counsellor
            giving nothing away.

Hippo

Go on you say, and hand me up the ladder, balanced
awkwardly in my tutu like some balletic hippo out of *Fantasia*
(which you probably never saw). Father told me, in the cinema
when he was six, that mouse magician scared the shit out of him.
Before mother, he smoked Gauloises coolly on a mountain top.
People change. You're not wearing your top hat, so I don't know
if this is real, or just a rehearsal. Behind us there is a dark forest
and sometimes a yellow veld, trees parasoled flat in the heat.
If I turn for a clear look, the sceneshifter drives it off in his truck.

Get in. The box is somewhat longer than my body, like a coffin
lined with white lace. Some wag has littered it with confetti.
It takes a certain mind to lie in a coffin and stay still. The box
is in three parts, painted with scenes and symbols: the pride
of lions, a murder of crows, two rings, and a constant moon.
There are parallel slots along the sides. I know what they are for.
This is where you'll plunge in the swords. These blades are real –
someone in the crowd has tested the steel bite against their tongue.
There is space for an axe between each joined segment of the box.

You will help me into this strange bed in my white dress and roses.
You'll smooth the hair from my face. So intimate, everyone will see.
You are ready with your axe. What tricks we will perform together!
I will lie down. I'll lie quite still with my arms loose, waiting
for a miracle. For something extraordinary to occur.
When a hippo dies, the whole crash gathers in the water, watched
by white oxpeckers. The herd nudges the dead, brown flanks
like a wedding silverside. Softly, they barge the corpse upriver
into the reeds. Then they begin licking. They lick the rough skin,
the hairs, the ear tips, its wounds. Nobody on earth can explain why.

Ballad

We didn't have swamp boots so we couldn't march out at dusk
to the marsh or wander the causeway, gathering fireflies into a jar.
We didn't have a stoop or back porch with weathered steps so
we couldn't sit under the stars and swig moonshine from a bottle,
talking of strangers we'd seen, their suitcases and sad black suits.

But some nights we did lie, stiff as a board, thinking of a peach tree
we'd dreamt of over the fence, sawn in half in our neighbour's yard
with its head propped up high on crutches next to its severed trunk
as though it were still a whole tree, the branches losing blossom,
a tire hung from the lowest limb, and some name carved in a heart.

And we did have a cabinet of curios (varnished shells, extracted teeth)
we'd pull out from the dust. We even had someone to bestow them on.
But they wouldn't know to hoard them under the fireflies and swamp
and moon as we do, or cradle them beneath the stars and half a tree
on the stoop of a warm night and think those times, those times weren't even

On Shells

I'm holding an egg, but not carefully.
My loose holding of an egg is directly related
to my understanding of its fragility.

*

We never cook together. You make scallops and
sea-spaghetti. It's impressive. I can't remember
if I just dream of telling you it's too ferulic.

*

I'm sure I dream of snails. I'm sending back
a snail too large to be consumed, even though
I'd never eat something so attached to its shell.

*

A shell is an evolutionary afterthought. How,
and indeed why, does a vulnerable body survive,
only to manufacture itself a far-too-thin wall?

*

I ruin the scallops by demanding reasons.
You don't have time to answer or cook to perfection.
If we cooked together. If we deshelled together.

*

Shells are both containers and barriers.
Keeping in and keeping out. They necessitate
portals, thresholds, nacre, and smashing.

*

Eggs are only fragile when dropped from a height
or stepped on sideways. Under vertical pressure
at the apex, they are remarkably resilient.

*

I'm not really even holding an egg. I'm holding
an image by Carrington of a giantess cradling an egg.
Her face is a waxed moon. Her back is to the sea.

*

You have been curled so long in your shell,
I don't believe you've noticed the deep scar
inside each scallop, or how metallic their roe.

*

I never learnt to cook except eggs. Granny made
starving look so easy. My notebooks are full up
with her, and with you. Yours are full of recipes.

*

Snails have to line up their shell-swirls to mate.
A left-coiled snail can never connect with a right.
Darling, we've been circling one another so long.

*

Eggs are wise. A splitting moon. They know when
to break open. Without feathers, blind-eyed –
they don't even wait for clear sight.

In the Black Square

After Kandinsky's 'Im schwartzen Viereck'

When I first received a poster of the painting, I stuck it to my bedroom door.
I looked at it every day and with care. Noticed the relationship
between subtle and strong palettes. The quiet tension
in the lines, like a mountain harp. The bold yellow a mountain sun.
I would pull my gaze up and down the lines like a mountain climb.
I would trace a landscape that wasn't there,
coming to rest on a small slice of blue: a jay's flight.

At some point, I framed the poster against a black background in a white frame.
I was pleased with this. The poster's edges were torn from house-moves.
Housing the poster, I felt, kept it safe and was also visually pleasing.
I hung the pleasingly-framed poster on the wall, of course.

I still looked at the painting, but now I also looked at the frame.
There was nothing wrong with that, with adding a relationship
between the frame and the lines in the painting; the delicate energy
of that sliced canvas, reprinted in probably more subtle pastel tones,
for poster form, than intended, now contained in a starker monochrome.

At some point, I obtained a number of prints by various artists
and pleasingly framed them in black or white frames and hung them on the walls
beside and opposite my framed Kandinsky poster. I still looked
at the poster of this painting, and also at these prints,
and increasingly also the frames of the prints and the way my house
was filling with frames. The frames of prints and posters were becoming
part of the walls of the house and I was starting to notice them only the way
you notice the walls of the house you live in. I'm not saying any of this
was a bad thing. From time to time, I would still stand quietly
in front of the Kandinsky, look through the glass, and see again
a relationship in the landscape that wasn't there.

At some point, I fell in love with a man. I looked at him every day and with care.

Still Life, A Translation

We've grown introspective, gazing so long at the Cyrillic
of our furnishings: the proud П of the dining table, the stiff-backed h,
the bureau's shut Д. We are trying to read our way out of these rooms.
They cancelled Russian before my class could learn.

Get me to an online course in Slavonic interior design!
Get me to a life drawing class for chaise longues!
Let me linger over their turned ankles, the curve of their backs.

Oh, for an old leather sofa, its cracked hide transcribing
hearthside proverbs. Play the balalaika, couch! Pull up a samovar,
second-hand stool, and dance – Калинка, калинка, калинка моя!
Kick up the wood-dust and moths and tell us what you mean
by standing all day in the same spot, and never breaking down.

Mother's Mother

Grandma slept with her eyes open,
made the walls and furniture disappear
through sheer willpower. Or as if
sight was a decision she stopped making.

Grandma believed tears were crocodile eggs
laid to snap at her ankles. *Watch yourself –*

she'd gasp, as though stung by salt.
Her veins were veiled under powder;
her skin broke on whatever it touched –

a satchel left in the hall, the leaf of a book.
You're so sharp you'll cut yourself.
I never thought of her as thin-skinned.

I dreamt a wild egg could take down
the swell of a cat's tit. A strange cure.

This is for those unwritten
lost by an open window, disappearing   behind blinds.

I was looking for you without trying
to see you –

                    even in the dark we avoided each other.

                    You spoke in half sentences and affronts.
                    Confronting mirrors, thinking about your mother,
                    your mother's mother.

You were peering into each room of your mother's house,
trying to go to sleep. Seeing again under closed lids
the marigolds from the kitchen window.

                              So much work year after year
                              and all the orange and yellow grief of it.

The roses staggering against the garage wall

                                             verging on collapse.

For Violet & unnamed.

'Pity for the loss of roses' – V. Woolf

Pity the violets shrunk, the pinks
shrivelled, the lost round
of peas from swelled pods.

The breathlessness of lungworts,
their phlegm-pale specks. The slips
of cows, their untouched teats
the spotted hollow of a foxglove, wanting
the bee's suck. Pity the busy bees,

the lace of old ladies, their green
fingers: a felled innocence

of snowdrops. A heart
of bleeding hearts. Of rue.

Rib

I snip the wires out of my bras.
     My ribs are trying to tell me something.
          Mostly they tell me I'm in pain.
               Sharp. Persistent as a mother, gasping
          like skirts snatched above a wave.
     Ribs! Aren't we both women? Curved,
bone-tired, under the lace and clasps?

Here is the actual pelvis of King Alfred,
     compacted by haemorrhoids. And this –
          Richard III's vertebrae, hissing with scoliosis.
               Reliquaries may be ornate as you please,
          angels fat with gilt and filigree, cradling
     a morsel of toe. Who's kept schtum
under a carpark, scattered like apple pips?

Everyone sees a grave as a stone house,
     and everyone brings warming gifts.
          Such life, body. Such pain, ribs. Don't think
               I haven't noticed. Flowers for your troubles!
          Daisies to push up through your spaces
     fixing their yellow eyes upon the sun,
like hands reaching, reaching from a boat.

Perdita

That day, I opened you up. Slid up your dress
and down your rough white knickers to find
a cavity in your plastic. A sprung hatch
like a submarine door / space-station airlock.
And inside: a tiny spindle, a switch clicking
uselessly; a moulded, purposeful void.

I took you down to Mother: once you'd held
a record player spinning miniature vinyl,
loops of laughter or gorgeous sobs, a mocking
comfort, replayed in play. Even, beating from
your belly, surreal jazz – birth-kick grooves.

Those records are outmoded, broken, misplaced,
and you have lost your voice. Your tipping blink
unsettled with a shake, I carefully re-dress you,
lift up my vest to press where my hatch must be.

At night, I replace you in the cot, a copy of my own
now long outgrown. *I'm here, I'm listening*, I say.
I hold and hold your plastic hand in mine.

Emergency

After Frank O'Hara

I love you. I love you,
but I'm turning to my verses
and my heart is closing
and opening instead a small valve,
a hatch over the wing.

I'm rolling out the rubber slide
like a yellow tongue
and everyone inside, panicking
and removing stilettos,
leaving their baggage locked
in the hold, one by one must file out

in an orderly line. Wheee!
Down the chute, crossing your arms
over your heart. Hug, hug
like a child's bear,

and into the sea, turning and freezing.
You've at least two more hours to live.

Songs the Owls Brought

i

We grow wise keeping quiet watch:
pale sentries doing the moon's work.

Feathers are not soft for stroking;
they are silencers, deadening night.

Our eyes are black moons. Meat saucers.
Small bones are a gag: hack them out.

Pellet the dark with skeleton pearls:
a collage of corpses; a machine gun in a copse.

Shrieks leap from us like ghost-owls
rending night's pavilion, calling hunger

or love. A fearful warning.

ii

I spent ten years breaking skin;
          each slice a beak, a shrieking flap.
I lied to my counsellor, my lover,
          the people I thought
were my mother, until
          a machine gun in my throat
coughed out all the spitelets stuck like bone.
          I tried to close each horrifying gape
with a new corpse but, fed, they called again –
                        again.
It was three thousand moons before I learnt
          hunger can both shriek and silence
& the starving hunter kills
          all cries quieter than ghosts,
beneath the rustle of fear in the grass,
          the quivering pitch of hope.

iii

Baby Owl, you are wise as night /knowing that morning will come.

Knowing night is nothing to fear /with your cool moon eyes.

That curled in eyeless shell there is no dark /no idea of breaking
/until the bounds
crack.

That knowledge is a line of fractured chalk /spanned wing parting thin
worlds.

Baby Owl, I love you:
/give me your night
/your soft absence of fear.

Flea Ear

It's so cold, the pigeons are headless: *wind your neck in!*
All I want for Christmas is to be able to unscrew my throat,
and tuck my head into the feral warmth of an underarm.

It'd need a good clear out, maybe with one of those Egyptian
embalming instruments for drawing the brain down the nose.
I'll tear your head off and spit in the hole! Scoop matted twigs
and feathers through the eye-sockets, shake out the lice,
the pests. The pigeons design new nests each spring, free
of parasites. No one's at their best during a flea infestation.

Let Kennard have the sonnets; give me Donne. I notice how bitten
I'm getting, living with you. Don't take it personally. This poison is
impartial as a turndown service. Beat up the duvet, out in the cold
so the marriage-bed can breathe. There's a bloody wing in the road.
Another mild dove bites the dust. Somewhere, a species is winning.

day of the cockroach

the day the cockroach came we fought nine times.
that week we mopped the floors, scoured the hob,
lugged the fridge from its sentry post, tossed away
the spiders, gagged on the sweetness of insecticide.

we set our careful traps; caught nothing. the pills of
poison lay untouched, crumbled like old love hearts.
be mine. sweet lips. i dreamt of mandibles nibbling
my eyelashes. cannibalistic limbs, invasive antennae

earwigging my thoughts, hooked, seismographic feet
measuring the tremor of my heart, assessing whether
to run or resist. they are not afraid when a harsh light
is turned on around them. invisible currents illumine

their world. the pressure of approach; a relay of soft
breath rippled through exoskeleton. their knowledge
is carboniferous. older than dance, or love. intuition
born of survival. they know when the jig is up, when

to hang on. i unpack my suitcase, refold socks. observe
your eyes at night encased like wings, switching back
and forth, watching imagined roaches raid our walls.
i warm cold feet against yours. listen through my soles.

I have been learning from mushrooms.

They teach me to look harmless & store poison.
They are grey women in caps & violent underskirts,
soft-boiled flesh spilling over the bark.

How fast these slow things move! Such agile decay unfurling
overnight. A village of minute rooftops caps the morning,
spoked like spinning wheels after a long sleep.

Ah, but they are certainly old women:
whose eaves survive the yearly tremors,
who keep a pot of water boiled
& linen presses full of herbs
& every girl in trouble
knows their name.

I don't know what I'm writing about but

it's always wanting to know moss.
It's been impossible to get an answer.

Wanting to touch whenever it's secret,
on a low wall or behind a tree. To cry
into its unresponsive green pillows at night.
Never lie face down on a mossed stone at night.

Moss is the smell of hunger. I imagine a moss throat.
I recall pregnant mothers, stories of eating dirt.
You went through a lot of gherkins. We joke
about how sharp I turned out. Give me soft to eat.
Never lick moss off a grave. The dead are entitled
to a mitigation of stone. Besides, it's full of woodlice.

Moss bristles like a whisper. That's the sporophytes.
You sporophyte through my dreams, hinting and soft.
I can't decipher you, so I spend twenty-two years prodding.
Ah love, time to turn off the waterworks.
Moss can hold twenty times its own weight in water.

Perhaps the healing properties of bog moss,
recorded at the Somme – *"Mosses At War!"* –
were known to me all along, deep in my limbic system.

God! For a cool plaster of moss applied to the frontal lobe.
"…after a transient attack, patients may not respond
appropriately. Emotions may be felt but not expressed."
Take your forehead off that moss henge. This is a heritage site.

It's not that I don't know how to pray. It's just too much
like whispering into moss and missing the whispers of moss.

A doctor opens her briefcase. In place of a stethoscope,
there are two wads of sphagnum. Repeat into peat:
What does it mean? What does it mean?
What does it mean? What does it mean?

Moss's refusal to respond lacks all defiance.
It is always gently and fully occupied.

Nasturtium

Words fell from your lips and curled on the ground
like worm casts crumbling in dry heat. Grandad cursed
the cracked clay of the front lawn and a hosepipe ban,
but mildly, as he eased peas from their shells or petted
gooseberries from their stems – as he did everything.

I wake restless and find raisins in my pocket, animal
brown and soft, secreting sweetly. I find afternoons
in mornings, and years just before midday, if it's quiet.
I find fruit in the strangest places: pips in my eyelids,
forgotten raspberries rotting on the bookshelves.

The compost's full and I'm afraid to cross the yard
in case I crush another snail, curled like a dropped
word in its useless shell. No case is hard enough.
It mounds up like your father's wheelbarrow full
of clippings. *Don't let Grandpa wheel you about*

laughing in the sun – the poor man's back is bad.
I didn't notice his smile fall to one side, or when
he started veering left. I didn't believe it was him
in those white sheets like a peeled leaf: he wasn't
a stark man. I think you expected your own droop

in a scientific sort of way. Like jewel nasturtiums
cannot be trusted year to year not to revert, red
back to yellow. Pepper mouths spitting up sunset.
Disappointment for *directions* was the surprise.
What turns up, searching. *Treatment* for *tongue.*

We don't speak of it now, or the hospital parking,
or silence under the damson trees, or recovery,
or your chart with *independent* underlined, or rot
kept quiet at the back of the veg patch, or February,
or the wheelbarrow's red ball rolling, like a setting sun.

my TV my city

the vegetable smell of unwashed hair I'm picking
courgette flowers under a walnut tree under a
rainbow with too much blue in it too much like
a city where I'm watching a TV chef picking his
courgette flowers under a walnut tree picturing
the charred smell of vegetables like hair I haven't
washed for days because of the TV in the city just
last week I was ready to leave you forever dear
city put out the blazing rows charring your streets
washed with blue light above too-bright courgettes
I cannot stop watching my TV my city oh he picked
me nowhere near a walnut tree I can't stop watching
unwashed because I cannot stop to pick so yellow
courgette flowers so fragile and so ready to burn

Jupiter

My horoscope invites me to interview next week.
Jupiter is expanding my horizons; he's never given me the time of day,
leaves that to the sun teasing the bedclothes. Stretching and yawning –
that's the easy bit. Mornings are always hard. The nights
are harder. I ought to apply myself more.

Jupiter has a mean radius of 43,440.7 miles.
Unreliable, as you might expect. Too big to be held
accountable, looming cheerfully from the wings like a Norwegian prince.
The sunlight lifts the blinds no more than a centimetre.
I shift, dreaming of uneaten food, a cloud of flies.

Jupiter offers rich wines from his store, a nebulous feast;
fortune favours the massive. My horoscope says: *Get ready to embrace*
the past. A gas giant is rising in the east. An unburnt star. Light up.
I'm not ready, Jupiter! I want to cry, but next door will know
I'm still in bed, not opening to anyone who knocks.

how small we are, how little we know.

in late august, the spiders take over the garden,
stringing it up like a terrace crossed with washing
come clean – *reenie, he didn't reel home last night.*

i don't mind – that fortnight watching the outside
get laced from behind my utility window,
the over-there of darkening summer leaves.

one hangs by the glass, legs drawn into an X,
marking time. a workforce of ghosts pencilling maps
between the fences: what do they hope to achieve,

tying the space together, or measuring its distance?

Victory

We razed a whole summer.
There was rubble everywhere.
The stop-motion movements of flies.

Through all of it, campanulas flowered,
their blue bells ringing like victory,
but one or other of us noticed only sometimes.

First I got sick to my stomach, then eczema,
then thrush. We didn't have sex
and that was the government's fault.
There is no one left to explain it to.

Perhaps, while our backs were turned
and our arms crossed, sharp-elbowed
rain pressed the campanulas into the dirt
promising it was for their own good,
or their lifted skirts burnt dry in the sun.

We only saw them perked, in the long evening light,
as if to ask what possibly we thought was wrong.

War and Peace

We were spending the night apart when I heard about Tolstoy
forgetting which character was which in the end.

What a relief it must have been!

All those Bezukhovs and Rostovs running away over the fields
swapping britches and skirts and patronyms, and whooping
through the snow. And hunting – of course on a hunt, but for what?
Prize wolfhounds tumbling into wolves in the brake
and where will the yapping and tails emerge with definitive form?

This is the kind of poem I would normally research
or fact-check in some way. Let it do as it pleases!

How good it feels to talk aloud in an empty house.

That's one way it could start:
Tolstoy muttering room to room; Tolstoy hunting
something, someone in the hall while alone one cold morning.
The window opening a flat sky like a diary.
Coals clicking under their tongues.

In bursts a visitor with gloves and wrinkled brow!
– *Natasha? Oh just a character, a draft,*
she's whispering at the window, you see…

Imagine him turning himself, themselves
into names and blushes, betrayals and letters, clubs
and card-sharps and dresses and dinners, horses, battalions
and bureaucrats, fears, compulsions, selfishness, marriage and debt.

All those people constructed, year after year
like statues of ice, or blocks of an ice palace
stacked up and frozen, like so much history.

And suddenly one day, imagine them melting –
edges all washed away, like the flood of a Russian spring!

A cool, forgetful torrent rushing through the woods and out,
into the dancing sun.
So much, so much forgiveness.

Acknowledgements

'Hippo' appeared in issue 44 of *The Moth* and was highly commended in the Forward Prize, published in the *Forward Anthology 2022*.

'You could see us falling even then.' appeared in *Under The Radar* issue 29.

'Mother's Mother' was shortlisted in the Live Canon poetry competition 2020 and appeared in their 2020 anthology.

'day of the cockroach' appeared in issue 71 of *The Interpreter's House*.

'Songs The Owls Brought' received special mention in the Against The Grain poetry competition 2019 and was published on their site.

'For Violet & unnamed' appeared in issue 92 of *The Rialto*.

lay out, your unrest.

www.ingramcontent.com/pod-product-compliance
Lightning Source LLC
Chambersburg PA
CBHW031636040426
42452CB00007B/849